Fangtastic RAPS

To Kate, Peter, George and Harriet,
with love
T.M.

ORCHARD BOOKS
338 Euston Road,
London NW1 3BH
Orchard Books Australia
Hachette Children's Books
Level 17/207 Kent Street, Sydney, NSW 2000
First published in Great Britain in 1998
First paperback publication in 1999
This edition published in 2004
Text © Tony Mitton 1998
Illustrations © Martin Chatterton 1998
The rights of Tony Mitton to be identified as the Author and
Martin Chatterton as the Illustrator of this Work have been asserted by
them in accordance with the Copyright, Designs and Patent Act, 1988.
A CIP catalogue record for this books is available from the British library.
1 84362 752 3
3 5 7 9 10 8 6 4 2
Printed in Great Britain

Fangtastic RAPS

Tony Mitton

Illustrated by Martin Chatterton

ORCHARD BOOKS

Try reading Scary Raps, Royal Raps, Big Bad Raps, Robin Hood Raps and Monster Raps next, or I'll bite your neck!

CONTENTS

Batty Rap

Once upon a time
in Transylvania -
you won't hear anything
crazier, zanier -

there lived a count
in a crumbling pile,
and it made you shudder
to see him smile.

His face was white
and his eyes were red,
and the story went
that he should've been dead.
But he hung around
in a long black cloak,
and it made you shiver
whenever he spoke.

Now, late at night,
when the moon was high,
he'd cruise around
as a bat, in the sky.

And wherever he flapped,
yes, wherever he flew,
the wolves cried, '*Howl!*'
and the owls called, '*Whoooo?*'

For he had two teeth
that were sharp and long,
and, really, for a bat,
he was rather strong.

But the thing that worried folk
most of all
was, whenever he could,
he'd pay them a call,
and while they were sleeping,
late at night,
he'd give their necks
a nasty bite.

Yes, he'd drink their blood
for a midnight feast,
so the folk all called him
'The Vampire Beast'.

He didn't like beans
and he didn't like eggs,

and he wouldn't even chew
on chicken legs.
He didn't like fish
and he'd never choose chips,
and he wouldn't let pasta
past his lips.

He didn't like ice-cream,
cake or jelly -
they disagreed
with his delicate belly.

And if he was offered
a chocolate biscuit,
he'd say with a sigh,
"I'd better not risk it.
To me all chocolate
tastes like mud...
so I'll just take a sip
of HUMAN BLOOD!"

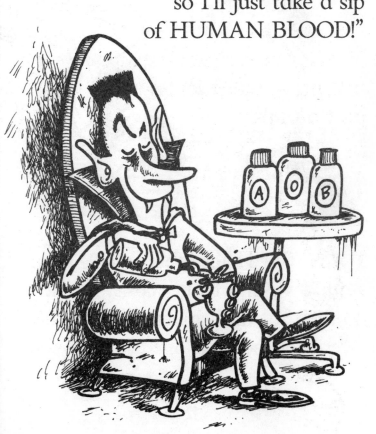

Now, folk round there
said it just wouldn't do,
but no one would dare
to tell him to shoo!

For he filled those folk
with awe and fear,
so they sat and shivered
over their beer.

But one day, travelling
through Transylvania,
there came a doctor,
braver and brainier,
who said, "I'll fix him
good and proper.
That count of yours
will come a cropper.

Just show me where
he likes to sleep
and I'll turn him into
a dusty heap."

Those folk were quick
to lead him where
that mean old vampire
had his lair,
where he slept in a coffin
in a room at the back,
at Hilltop Castle,
Home of Drac.

Now, he always went
to bed at dawn
and he kept his curtains
tightly drawn,
for he wouldn't let any
sunlight in.
"It's bad," he'd say,
"for my delicate skin."

So, in marched dauntless
Doctor John,
with a string of smelly
onions on.
(Dear me, did I
forget to say
that onions drive
a Drac away?)

Said John, "These onions
really smell.
They'll make him choke
and cough and yell.

They may even make
that cruel count cry.
Come to think of it -
so will I!"

But though his eyes
shed many a tear,
he didn't give way
to the tug of fear.

He creaked the door
and he walked right in.
The Count got up
with a grisly grin,
saying, "Come in here
my boy, and by heck,
I'll hold you tight
and I'll bite your neck!"

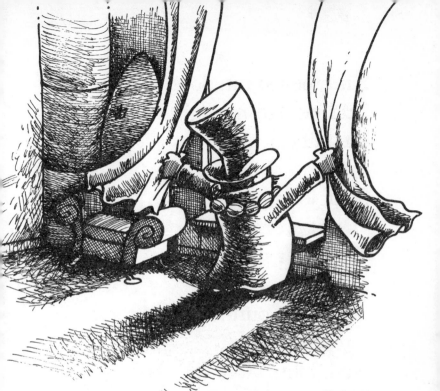

But Doctor John,
without delay,
went marching up
to the window bay,
and he pulled those curtains
open wide,
and the golden sunlight
streamed inside.

19

Said the Count,
"Oh no, it'll make
me blind!"

Said John,
"Don't worry.
We won't mind."

Said the Count, "It'll turn me
into dust."
Said John, "OK, Count,
if you must..."
And as the folk
peered through the door,
this is the sight
that they all saw.

The Count had crumbled
into a pile,
till all that was left
was his spooky smile.
And the words that came
from those leering lips
were, "OK, guys,
I've had my chips.

But, just remember,
my name's Drac.
You've won this time,
but I'll be back!"

21

The folk all gave
one mighty whoop.
Then they all went home
for onion soup.

And they set up a statue
of Doctor John,
with a great big bunch
of onions on.

So if you ever travel
to Transylvania,
land of mists,
where the weather's rainier,
string some onions,
good and strong,
and garlic too
for a powerful pong.

And remember this:
it ain't no joke
to talk about bats
or wear a cloak.

Hi there, kids.
It's me. I'm back.
Did you dig the story
of Old Count Drac?

Well, here's a tale
a whole lot hairier.
It comes from a place
they call Bavaria.
The story happens
in a deep, dark wood.

Are you sitting comfortably?
Nice. Good.

You remember that dude,
the woodcutter man,
who helped Red Riding Hood
and her gran?
Well, something that story
forgets to say,
is when he chased
that wolf away,

it gave him a scratch
and a bit of a bite,
and after that
he didn't feel right.

But he shrugged and swaggered
and bravely said,
"It's OK, honeys,
I ain't dead.
It's just a nip
and a bit of a graze.
I ain't gutted.
Nope. No ways."

But as he set off
through the wood,
he knew he didn't
feel so good.

And after he had
said goodbye,
he thought he heard
a howling cry.
It made his skin
begin to prickle.
And then his toes
began to tickle.

His gut began
to throb and ache.
"I guess I guzzled
too much cake."

He scratched his head
and rubbed his beard.
"Strange," he muttered.
"I feel weird.

I seem to want
to holler and howl."
By now his voice
was a grumbly growl.
"I wonder what's
gone wrong with me.
Was there something
in my tea?

What's the reason?
What's the cause?
Holy hot dogs!
I've got paws!"

His eyes went wide
in a crazy stare,
for his palms were sprouting
bristly hair.

His body bulged
and wouldn't stop.
His buttons burst off -
PIP! and *POP!*

His head began
to whizz and sing.
Then suddenly
his belt snapped - *PING!*

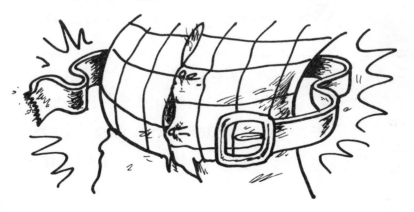

Then the woodman gave
a mighty wail:
"Howling horrors!
I've grown a tail!

My clothes have burst.
I'm nude. I'm bare.
Thank goodness, then,
for all this hair."

He kicked his boots off,
leaped on a log.
"Owoooh!" he hollered.
"I'm a dog!

But not a mutt
that's meek and mild.
I'm a wolf.
I'm really wild.
I ain't no spaniel,
soft and sad.
I'm a savage beast -
I'm bad!"

Beside the log
was a forest pool.
He saw himself
and whispered, "Cool!
I'm tired of being
good and brave.
Now it's time
to misbehave."

By now the moon
was big and bright.
It filled his blood
with wild delight.
He raved and romped
right through the wood,
doing things
that no one should.

As simple folk
sat watching telly,
his howling made them
shake like jelly.

The Three Little Pigs
and Mother Goose
shrieked, "Help! A werewolf's
on the loose."
And just to show
how he was tough,
he blew their house down
with one puff.

But Woodman Wolf
had a better idea.
"Hah!" he snarled
with a wicked leer.

"I'll gobble up Red
and gulp her gran.
Just watch me work
my wolfish plan."

He went to the house
where Gran and Red
had snuffed their lamp
and gone to bed.

He bashed the door
and broke it down.
Old Gran got up
with a yawn and a frown.
And before he could start
his werewolf meal,
"Down, boy, down," she snapped.
"To heel!"

"And don't you dare
to howl and holler,"
she added, fitting
a lead and collar.

"This looks to me
like a werewolf fit.
So just stay cool now.
Sit, boy, sit."

For Gran was old
and Gran was wise,
(and Gran had met
all kinds of guys).

And just as many
a story tells,
old women in woods
work magic spells.

She went to her cupboard
(which wasn't bare).
"Hmmm," she crooned.
"Removing hair..."

She scratched her head
and took a pause.
"Mmmm," she hummed.
"Reducing claws..."

She rubbed her chin
and had a think.
"Ah," she sang.
"A tail to shrink..."

"Hum," she murmured.
"Wolf to man...
Mix these gently
in my pan.

Now add a dash
of Diet Whizz—"
The mixture hissed,
and seemed to fizz.

"There," she sighed,
"that ought to do.
Here, now, Wolfman,
drink this brew."

She put the potion
to his lips.
He drank it down
in little sips.

And when he'd polished
off the pan -
bingo! There he was:
a man!

"What's going on?"
said Little Red,
as round the door
she poked her head.
"Why's Woody here?
And why's he nude?
Really! This seems
rather rude.

Remember, we're a
children's book.
Let's get him dressed
before they look.
Now, children, please don't
peer and stare,
while I get Woody
some clothes to wear."

45

Then Gran got up
and warmed the pot,
as Woody Wolfman
told the lot,
of how he'd turned
to wolf from man
and tried to gobble
dear old Gran,

and how she'd mixed
a magic spell
to turn him back
and make him well.

But now, my dears,
the story's read.
It's time to stumble
off to bed.

Try not to think
of biting beasts
and all their gooey,
gory feasts.

Ah, see, the moon
shines round and bright.
It fills me with
such high delight.
I have to fly now.
Bye. Goodnight.